MINDFULNESS IN SPORTS

BY AMBER BULLIS, MLIS

BLUE OWL
BOOKS

TIPS FOR CAREGIVERS

Social and emotional learning (SEL) helps children manage emotions, learn how to feel empathy, create and achieve goals, and make good decisions. An important goal of teaching SEL skills is to provide students with the skills to process and regulate their emotions, learn problem-solving skills, and make good decisions. Playing sports requires many of these same skills.

BEFORE READING

Talk to the reader about how sports can make him or her feel.

Discuss: Do you like playing sports? Do you ever get worried or nervous when you play? How does your mind feel when you play sports?

AFTER READING

Talk to the reader about mindfulness and sports.

Discuss: What does it mean to be mindful when you play sports? What are some ways you can practice mindfulness to help you enjoy sports more?

SEL GOAL

Students are likely to be motivated to learn mindfulness techniques if they can see how they will benefit their performance in sports. For example, when students learn ways to use breathing to calm down, it can positively impact high-pressure situations during sporting events. This technique can also be used in the classroom. Use this motivation to encourage kids to practice different mindfulness techniques.

TABLE OF CONTENTS

CHAPTER 1

WHAT IS MINDFULNESS?

The score is tied. You are the next batter up. You want to get a hit. But you think about the last time you struck out. This is the perfect time to practice **mindfulness**!

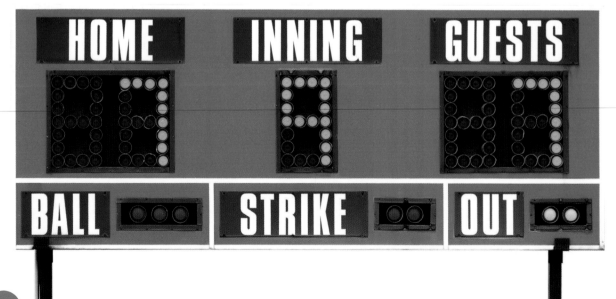

Pause to **focus** on your thoughts. Focus on the present moment and hitting the ball. Tell yourself you can do it!

Do you ever feel nervous or **anxious** when you play sports? You don't want to disappoint your team. Your parents are watching. You want to make them proud. Mindfulness can help you let go of worries.

PLAY WITH INTENTION

What do you like about playing sports? Do you play because they are fun or because it feels good to win? Find your reason. Whether you play on a team or **compete** on your own, play with **intention**.

CHAPTER 2

HOW IT HELPS

Sports are good for your body and mind. Being active gives your body exercise. It can help you sleep better, too!

Playing sports helps you set **goals** and **achieve** them. This can build your **self-esteem**. You can also make friends in sports! You play with people who have similar interests.

Being mindful means taking care of your body. Take breaks to check on how you feel. You notice you feel thirsty. You take time to drink more water.

If you feel short of breath, focus on your breathing. **Inhale** deep through your nose. **Exhale** out of your mouth.

SET GOALS!

Notice how your body feels after each practice or game. Can you push yourself a little more? What is a goal you could work toward?

Did you wipe out on your last run? Close your eyes and breathe deeply. Let your mistakes go. When the gate drops, you are ready. You are focused on the present. You do well on this run!

Our bodies and physical abilities play a big role in sports. But it's important to focus on your mind, too.

There are a lot of people watching. It is hot out, and you are tired. It is time to focus. Drown out the noise of the crowd. Think back to practice. Remember what your coach taught you. You are ready! You focus on the play your team planned.

CHAPTER 3

PRACTICE IT!

It is game day. Someone shouts that your team will lose. You want to shout back. Instead, you pause to think about the best decision. You are in charge of your thoughts.

You block out the shouting and focus on the game. You protect the goal! You feel proud.

It's time to perform your **routine**. You feel nervous. You want to perform well.

You run through it in your mind. You remember the steps. You have practiced them over and over. You are **confident** and ready! You nail it!

Being mindful can help you be a better teammate, too! Your teammate didn't pass you the ball. You know you could have made the shot.

Another teammate shoots and scores. You take time to realize you are playing for the team. You tell your teammates they did a good job!

BE A GOOD SPORT

Support your teammates and cheer them on. Respect your coaches and **opponents**. Even if you lost, what did you learn?

GOALS AND TOOLS

GROW WITH GOALS

There are many ways to practice mindfulness in sports.

Goal: Show your teammates how to practice mindfulness! Being mindful can help your whole team stay focused on the same goal.

Goal: Talk to your coach! Maybe the whole team can do a mindfulness practice together before each game.

Goal: Practice mindfulness during the school day! Being mindful can help you perform better on the field and in the classroom.

Goal: Try different ways to practice mindfulness! Ask your librarian to help you research or find a book.

MINDFULNESS EXERCISE

Try to focus on your senses before and after practice or a game. Find a quiet place to close your eyes. Inhale through your nose. Exhale through your mouth. Focus on everything your senses are feeling.

1. How does your body feel? Does anything feel sore or tired?

2. How does your mind feel? What did you achieve today?

3. What do you feel grateful for? What is something positive that happened today?

GLOSSARY

achieve
To do something successfully
after making an effort.

anxious
Worried or very eager
to do something.

compete
To try hard to outdo others
at a task, race, or contest.

confident
Self-assured and having a strong
belief in your own abilities.

exhale
To breathe out.

focus
To concentrate on something.

goals
Things that you aim to do.

inhale
To breathe in.

intention
Something you mean to do.

mindfulness
A mentality achieved by focusing
on the present moment and calmly
recognizing and accepting your
feelings, thoughts, and sensations.

opponents
People or teams you play
or compete against.

routine
A practiced sequence of actions.

self-esteem
A feeling of personal pride
and respect for yourself.

TO LEARN MORE

FACT SURFER

Finding more information is as easy as 1, 2, 3.

1. Go to www.factsurfer.com

2. Enter "**mindfulnessinsports**" into the search box.

3. Choose your cover to see a list of websites.

INDEX

Blue Owl Books are published by Jump!, 5357 Penn Avenue South, Minneapolis, MN 55419, www.jumplibrary.com

Copyright © 2020 Jump! International copyright reserved in all countries. No part of this book may be reproduced in any form without written permission from the publisher.

Library of Congress Cataloging-in-Publication Data

Names: Bullis, Amber, author.
Title: Mindfulness in sports / by Amber Bullis.
Description: Blue Owl Books. | Minneapolis, MN: Jump!, Inc., [2020]
Series: Mindful me | Includes index. | Audience: Ages 7–10
Identifiers: LCCN 2019022750 (print)
LCCN 2019022751 (ebook)
ISBN 9781645271789 (hardcover)
ISBN 9781645271796 (paperback)
ISBN 9781645271802 (ebook)
Subjects: LCSH: Sports—Psychological aspects—Juvenile literature.
Mindfulness (Psychology)—Juvenile literature.
Classification: LCC GV706.4 .B83 2020 (print)
LCC GV706.4 (ebook) | DDC 796.01/9–dc23
LC record available at https://lccn.loc.gov/2019022750
LC ebook record available at https://lccn.loc.gov/2019022751

Editor: Jenna Trnka
Designer: Molly Ballanger

Photo Credits: 3bugsmom/iStock, cover; OcusFocus/iStock, 1; kdshutterman/Shutterstock, 3; Lane V. Erickson/Shutterstock, 4; Image Source/iStock, 5; HRAUN/iStock, 6–7; DnDavis/Shutterstock, 8; kali9/iStock, 9; nycshooter/iStock, 10–11; homydesign/Shutterstock, 12–13; Steve Skjold/Alamy, 14–15; Robo Michalec/Shutterstock, 16, 17; Image Source/Getty, 18–19; SDI Productions/iStock, 20–21.

Printed in the United States of America at Corporate Graphics in North Mankato, Minnesota.